165

Christmas Jokes For Kids

What do you call an elf who sings?

A wrapper!

What do you call people who are afraid of Santa?

Claustrophobic

What do you call an obnoxious reindeer?

Rude-olph

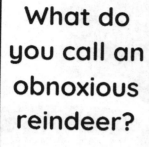

Why was Santa's little helper so sad?

Because he had low elf esteem!

What nationality is Santa Claus?

North Polish

Why does Santa Claus go down the chimney on Christmas Eve?

Because it soots him.

Why are Christmas trees so fond of the past?

Because the present's beneath them.

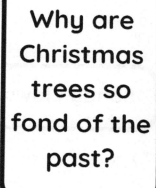

What do you call a broke Santa?

Saint Nickel Less

What do you call a cat on the beach at Christmas time?

Sandy Claws

What has 34 legs, 9 heads and 2 arms?

Santa Claus and his reindeer

Who doesn't eat on Christmas?

The turkey because it's already stuffed!

Why shouldn't you pick a fight with Santa?

Because he has a black belt.

What are Santa's little helpers called?

Subordinate clauses

Why is it always cold during Christmas?

Because Christmas is in Decemburrrr.

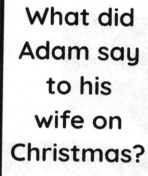

What did Adam say to his wife on Christmas?

It's Christmas, Eve!

24...

How does Santa get his reindeer to fly?

He makes them drink Red Bull to give them wings!

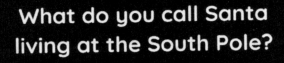

What do you call Santa living at the South Pole?

A lost clause

How did Darth Vader know what Luke got for Christmas?

He felt his presents.

What do you call a frog hanging from the ceiling?

Mistletoad

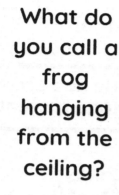

What do you get when you cross a snowman and a vampire?

Frostbite

Why was Santa cast in a musical?

He had great stage presents!

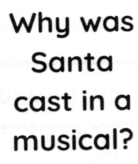

What do you call a sheep that doesn't like Christmas?

Baaaaaa humbug

Where do snowmen go to dance?

The snowball

What do you call a blind reindeer?

I have no eye deer!

What do you call it when you cut down a Christmas tree?

Christmas Chopping

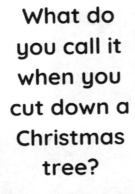

What do you call a singing elf with sideburns?

Elfis

What do you call a scary reindeer?

A scariboo

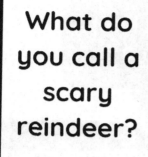

What do you call a wet deer?

A raindeer

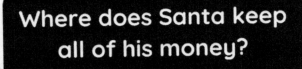

Where does Santa keep all of his money?

In a snow bank.

What do you call Santa when he's smelly?

Farter Christmas

What do you call Santa if he also lives at the South Pole?

Bipolar

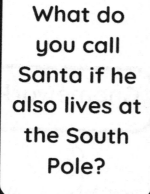

What do you call the wrapping paper left over from opening presents?

The Christmess

What did the little elves have to do when they got back from school?

Gnomework

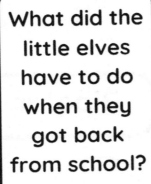

Who delivers Christmas presents to dogs?

Santa Paws

What cars do elves drive?

Toy-otas

What is a turkey's favorite dessert?

Peach gobbler

Who gives presents to cats on Christmas?

Santa Claws

What do you call buying a piano for the holidays?

Christmas Chopin

What do you learn at Santa's Helper School?

The elfabet

Where does Santa stop for hot chocolate?

Star-bucks

What do reindeer hang on their Christmas trees?

Hornaments

What do you call a snowman that can walk?

A snow-mobile

What do hip hop artists do on Christmas?

Unwrap

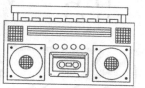

What does a squirrel see on Christmas Day?

The Nutcracker

How is Drake like an elf?

Because he spends all his time wrapping!

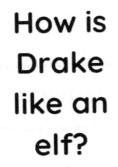

Where does Santa stay on vacations?

A ho ho ho-tel

What did Santa say to Mrs.Clause?

It's going to rein-deer!

What do you call a shark that delivers toys on Christmas?

Santa Jaws

What are you giving Mom and Dad for Christmas?

A list of everything I want.

What do snowmen like to do on the weekend?

Chill out.

What is a popular winter activity to do inside during the winter time?

Snow and Tell

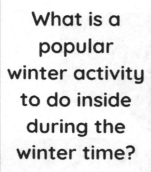

What do you get when you cross a Christmas tree with an Apple product?

A pine-apple

What do road crews use at the North Pole?

Snow cones

Where do polar bears vote?

The North Poll

What's the difference between Santa's reindeer and a knight?

One slays the dragon and the other's draggin' the sleigh!

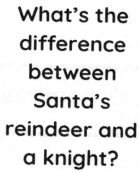

What do fish sing during Christmas?

Christmas corals

What is a Christmas tree's favorite candy?

Ornamints

What always comes at the end of December?

The letter R

What do you call a reindeer that wears ear muffs?

Anything you want! He can't hear you!

What do turkeys on space stations say?

Hubble, hubble

What does Santa say at the start of a race?

Ready, set, ho ho ho!

What did one snowman say to the other?

Do you smell carrots?

What did the reindeer say to the football player?

Your Blitzen days are over!

How does a sheep say Merry Christmas?

Fleece Navidad

What does the gingerbread man put on his bed?

Cookie sheets

In what year does New Year's Day come before Christmas Day?

Every year

What do snowmen eat for breakfast?

Frosted Flakes

How does a snowman lose weight?

He waits for the weather to get warmer!

Why does Santa work at the North Pole?

Because the penguins kicked him out of the South!

When does Christmas come before Thanksgiving?

In the dictionary.

What do you call a turkey fumbling the ball in football?

A fowl play

Why did the Christmas tree go to the barber?

He needed a trim.

Why was Frosty kicked out of the grocery store's produce section?

Because he got caught pickin' his nose!

Why did the man throw the butter out the window on Christmas eve?

Because he wanted to see the butterfly!

Why did the snowman tell his wife that his birthday cake tasted like a booger cake?

Because it was a carrot cake!

How do frogs open their Christmas presents?

Rippit. Rippit.

What's the difference between the normal and Christmas alphabet?

The Christmas one has Noel.

What does a turkey like to eat on Christmas?

Nothing – it's already stuffed.

What goes oh oh oh?

Santa walking backwards!

Why did Santa plant 3 gardens?

So he could ho ho ho!

What do witches sing for Christmas?

Deck the halls with poison ivy! Fa la la la la la la la!

What was the gingerbread man's reason for visiting the doctor?

He said he felt a little crumby!

What did the gingerbread man get when he broke his leg?

A candy cane

How do you greet a snowman?

By saying, "Chilly to meet you!"

What sound does a turkey's phone make?

Wing wing

What do you call a cat in the desert?

Sandy Claws

Why do Prancer and Blitzen get so many coffee breaks?

Because they are Santa's star-bucks!

What do you get when you cross a pig and Christmas tree lights?

A piglet

What do you get when Santa goes down the chimney when it's still lit?

Crisp cringle

How do you say no way during Christmas?

Snow way

What do you call a snowman with six pack abs?

The Abdominal Snowman

How do snowmen get to work?

By icicle

What do chickens mail their Christmas cards in?

Henvelopes

What song did the town sing when Belle and the Beast broke up?

Single Belle, single belle, single all the way!

How many cranberries grow on a bush?

All of them.

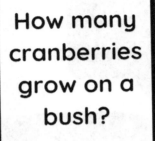

What happens when a Christmas tree gets a present?

He lights up!

Why were the reindeer mad at the elves?

Because they were being elf-ish!

Why doesn't Santa let his elves work on his computer?

Because they delete all of his Christmas cookies.

What comes at the end of Christmas Day?

The letter Y

What happens if you eat Christmas decorations?

You get tinselitus!

What do you call Santa when he stops moving?

Santa Pause

What's another breakfast cereal option for snowmen?

Snowflakes

What happened to the thief who stole a Christmas calendar?

He got 12 months!

What is a cow's favorite holiday?

Moo Years Day

What do sheep say to each other on Christmas?

Merry Christmas to ewe!

What is an elf's favorite sport?

North-pole vaulting

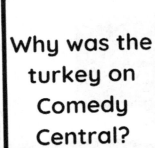

Why was the turkey on Comedy Central?

He was looking to get roasted.

What does a turkey drink from?

A gobble-t

What do snowmen take when they start getting too hot?

A chill pill

Who delivers presents to elephants on Christmas?

Elephanta Claus

How does Rudolph know Christmas is coming?

By checking his calen-deer!

What do you call a greedy elf?

Elfish

Why wouldn't the Christmas tree stand up?

It had no legs.

Why didn't Rudolph get a good report card?

Because he went down in history!

What kind of balls don't bounce?

Snowballs

What did one snowman say to the other?

You're cool!

What is every parent's favorite Christmas carol?

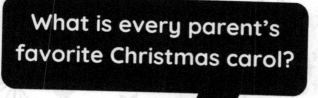

Silent Night

What's the name of Santa's detective brother?

Santa Clues

What falls in the winter but never gets hurt?

Snow

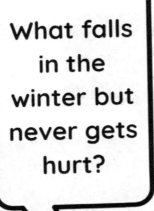

What do you get when you cross Christmas and a duck?

Christmas quackers

What does Santa use for measurements?

Santameters

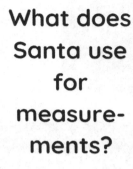
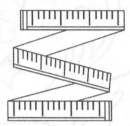

What happens when you cross ice and Christmas?

A cold Christmas!

What do monkeys sing at Christmas?

Jungle Bells

Which elf steals wrapping material from the rich and gives it to the poor?

Ribbon Hood

How did Santa Claus open the front door?

By using a tur-key!

What did the T-Rex say on Christmas Day?

Merry T-Rexmas

Which motorcycle does Santa ride?

A Holly Davidson

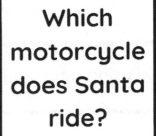

What is the best Christmas present in the world?

A broken drum, you just can't beat it!

What's white and goes up?

A confused snowflake

What is green, white and red all over?

A sunburnt elf

What do you call an old snowman?

Water

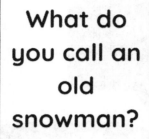

How many presents can Santa fit into an empty sack?

Only one because it's not empty after that!

What's Santa's dog's name?

Santa Paws

Where do snowmen go to dance?

A snow ball

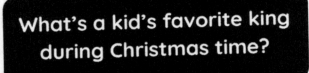

What's a kid's favorite king during Christmas time?

A stoc-king

What's an ig?

An eskimo's house without the loo!

How does a
cow like to
say Merry
Christmas?

Moowy
Christmas

What do snowmen call
their kids?

Chill-dren

What does a zombie get when he's late for a date?

The cold shoulder

Where do Christmas plants go to become movie stars?

Holly-wood

How do Christmas angels greet each other?

By saying, "Halo!"

What did the ghost say to Santa?

I'll have a boo Christmas without you.

What's red and white and keeps falling down chimneys?

Santa Klutz

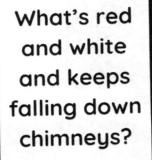

What did the peanut butter say to the grape during the holidays?

Tis' the season to be jelly!

What do sheep say to shepherds during Christmas?

Season's bleatings!

Where do you find reindeer?

Depends on where you leave em'!

Who is a Christmas tree's favorite singer?

Spruce Springsteen

How did Scrooge win the football game?

The ghost of Christmas passed!

What language does Santa speak?

North Polish

What do reindeer say before telling their best jokes?

This will sleigh you!

Why did the couple get married on Christmas eve?

So they could have a Merry-d Christmas!

Knock Knock!
Who's there?
Mary and Abby!
Mary and Abby who?
Mary Christmas and an Abby New Year!

Knock Knock!
Who's there?
Tissue.
Tissue who?
All I want for Christmas Tissue!

Knock Knock!
Who's there?
Hannah!
Hannah who?
Hannah partridge in a pear tree!

Knock Knock!
Who's there?
Murray
Murray who?
Murray Christmas
to all!

Knock Knock!
Who's there?
Gladys
Gladys Who?
Gladys Christmas!
Aren't you?

Knock Knock!
Who's there?
Dexter.
Dexter who?
Dexter halls with boughs of holly!

Knock Knock!
Who's there?
Phillip.
Phillip who?
Phillip my stockings with gifts!

Knock Knock!
Who's there?
Holly.
Holly who?
Holly-days are
here again!

Knock Knock!
Who's there?
Essen!
Essen who?
Essen it fun to listen
to these Christmas
jokes!

Knock Knock!
Who's there?
Iran!
Iran who?
Iran over here to get some presents!

Knock Knock!
Who's there?
Doughnut!
Doughnut who?
Doughnut open till Christmas Day!

Knock Knock!
Who's there?
Snow.
Snow who?
Snow use! I've forgotten my name again!

Merry Christmas!

Leave Your Feedback on Amazon

Please think about leaving some feedback via a review on Amazon. It may only take a moment, but it really does mean the world for small businesses like mine.

Even if you did not enjoy this title, please let us know the reason(s) in your review so that we may improve this title and serve you better.

From the Publisher

Hayden Fox's mission is to create premium content for children that will help them expand their vocabulary, grow their imaginations, gain confidence, and share tons of laughs along the way.

Without you, however, this would not be possible, so we sincerely thank you for your purchase and for supporting our company mission.

27000363R00050